P IS FOR PURR

CAROLE GERBER

Illustrations by
SUSANNA COVELLI

Published by Familius LLC, www.familius.com
PO Box 1249, Reedley, CA 93654

Familius books are available at special discounts for bulk purchases,
whether for sales promotions or for family or corporate use. For more
information, contact Familius Sales at orders@familius.com.

Library of Congress Control Number: 2022937061

Print ISBN 978-1-64170-741-1
Ebook ISBN 978-1-64170-768-8
KF 978-1-64170-778-7
FE 978-1-64170-788-6

Printed in China

Edited by Maggie Wickes and Erin R. Lund
Cover design by Carlos Guerrero
Book design by Brooke Jorden

10 9 8 7 6 5 4 3 2 1

First Edition

To Simon, who purred his way into my heart.

*I'm only a cat
and we'll get along fine . . .
as long as you know
I'm not yours . . . you're all mine!*
—Anonymous

Sailors brought the ancestors of American shorthairs on ships to guard the stored food.

A is for **AMERICAN**—the shorthaired, friendly cats that crossed the sea on sailing ships and kept them free of rats.

B is for each **BREED** of cat. A breed defines the way a feline looks, the way it sounds, and how it likes to play.

There are 45 breeds of pedigreed cats. A pedigree shows the line of ancestors a cat came from.

Cats' claws grow on the last bone of the toes on their front and back paws.

C is for the **CLAWS** attached to each cat's padded feet.
Cats use their claws to dig and climb and capture mice to eat.

D is for **DOMESTIC** cats that live with us at home.
They're related to big jungle cats—
but leave *those* cats alone!

Pet cats are descendants of African wildcats that once roamed the earth.

E is for the **EYES** of cats. Their round orbs are unique.
Even in the lowest light, cats find the things they seek.

Cats' eyes have adapted over time to see well in dim light so they can sneak up on their prey.

A cat's fur covers and protects its skin from heat and cold.

F is for the **FUR** on cats
that covers them like clothes.
Sometimes it sheds,
sometimes it mats,
but back it always grows!

GROOMING is how cats spruce up. That's the letter **G**.
All cats enjoy indulging in a daily cleaning spree.

Cats are tidy animals and will lick themselves clean when their fur gets dirty.

A cat always turns its head in response to sounds—even ones human ears cannot hear.

H is for the feline's **HEAD**, so big and wide and round.
A cat will turn it right away when it hears any sound.

I is for **INTELLIGENCE.**
Cats are cunning and they're smart.
They all know how to get their way
and creep into your heart.

The parts of cats' brains are connected in exactly the same ways as human brains.

JAWS of cats are powerful.
That's the letter **J**.
Cats use their jaws to grab,
subdue, and hold onto their prey.

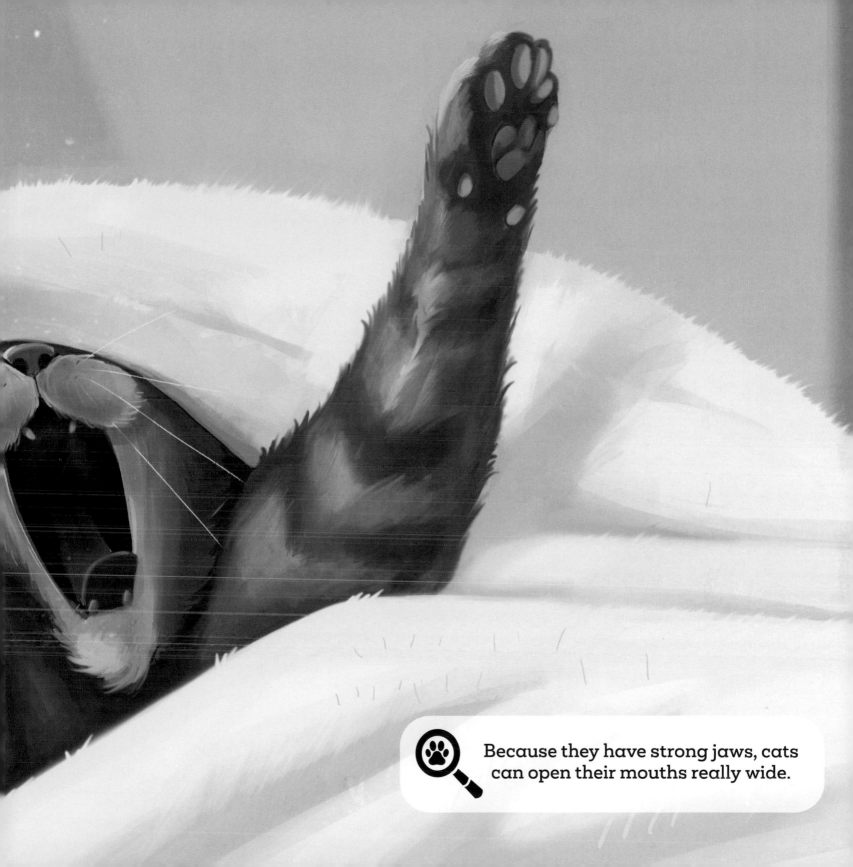

Because they have strong jaws, cats can open their mouths really wide.

A cat might have as few as one or as many as 10+ kittens at a time. But on average, a litter size is 3–6 kittens.

K is KITTENS.
Kitty cats are always born in litters.
Their lives depend on mother's milk,
for they are helpless critters.

L is for the **LITTER BOX**
that every feline needs
to carry out—then cover up—
its daily potty deeds.

er box

To train a cat, put it in a box filled with clean litter immediately after it eats.

Siamese cats "talk" a lot. They meow more and are louder than most other breeds.

M is **MEOW**. It's how cats talk—
and some talk a great deal!
Some meow all day.
Some meow at night.
Some meow before each meal.

NO ONE can boss a feline—that's the letter **N**.
Cats will do just what they choose, so take it with a grin.

Cats are independent, but they are also smart, loyal, and loving.

O is **ODOR**—nasty smells.
Cats keep their bodies clean,
and will not use a stinky box.
Instead, they leave the scene.

Cats require clean litter boxes
that are far away from their
bowls of food and water.

P is PURR. It shakes cats' fur. It's sweeter than a meow. It often shows contentment that says *I am happy now*!

Q is **QUICK**. A plain house cat runs thirty miles an hour—
and when it stops, it doesn't pant or even need a shower.

Cats have great balance.
If they fall, they twist their bodies
and land on their feet.

R is **ROUGH**. A feline tongue
works like a rough washrag.
Without a fuss, its tongue licks dust.
A cat will seldom gag.

A cat's tongue is rough because
of tiny bumps that stick up
on its surface.

SPHYNX is a naked, hairless cat. It's the letter **S**.
When it shivers, does it wish for fur like all the rest?

T is **TOES**. On its back paws, a cat has only four.
On each front paw, to help it climb, the feline has one more.

With 4 toes on each back foot and 5 on each front foot, cats have a total of 18 toes.

UNDERBELLY, soft and warm. That's the letter U.
A belly turned up on display is your cat's petting cue.

Cats often lie on their backs when they want to be petted—though not necessarily on the belly. It is a sign of trust.

V is **VET**, a pet doctor, who keeps cats safe from disease. Vets give vaccinations and also check cats for fleas.

 Vaccinations keep cats from catching deadly diseases and spreading them to humans.

W is **WHISKERS.**
They grow mainly on the
face, and help a cat to feel its
way into every space.

Whiskers grow beside a cat's nose, above the eyes, on cheeks, and on the backs of front paws.

X is **XANTHUS AV JOSTEDALSBREEN**, a Norwegian forest cat, once voted tops in England. Meow! How about *that*?

Xanthus was once voted "best in show" by the British Championship Norwegian Forest Cat Club.

Yankee cats are a breed called Maine coon. They are great hunters, but also friendly and gentle.

Y is for the **YANKEE** cat, that coon feline from Maine.
It's our native breed of cat and has a hunter's brain.

Z is for the **ZIBELINE**, a stocky cat that sees
through beautiful, expressive eyes.
It's also called "Burmese."

Zibeline **means "like the sable." It's a good name for these dark brown cats.**

Bibliography

A: "American Shorthair," *Cat Breed Guide*, Trupanion, https://trupanion.com/breeds/cat/american-shorthair.

B: "CFA Cat Breeds," The Cat Fanciers' Association, https://cfa.org/breeds/.

C: Wells, Virginia. "Structure and Function of the Claw and Foot Pad in Cats," *Pet Place*, August 3, 2015, https://www.petplace.com/article/cats/pet-health/structure-and-function-of-the-claw-and-foot-pad-in-cats/.

D: Hamper, Beth. "The Unique Metabolic Adaptations and Nutrient Requirements of the Cat," African Wildcat, from *Felines of the World*, 2020, ScienceDirect, https://tinyurl.com/2p83hmma

E: Syufy, Frannie. "Cats and Their Very Unique Eyes," *The Spruce Pets*, updated July 12, 2021, https://www.thesprucepets.com/guide-to-cat-eyes-552114.

F: Wells, Virginia. "Structure and Function of the Skin and Hair Coat in Cats," *PetPlace*. August 3, 2015. https://www.petplace.com/article/cats/pet-health/structure-and-function-of-the-skin-and-hair-coat-in-cats/

G: Shojai, Amy. "Why Do Cats Lick and Groom Themselves So Often?" Cats, Cats Behaviour & Training, *The Spruce Pets*, updated March 16, 2022, https://www.thesprucepets.com/why-cats-groom-themselves-so-often-4126526.

H: Arnold, Brooke. "Play This Sound that Only Your Cat Can Hear!" Awesome Stories, *The Cattington Post*, posted July 21, 2021, https://catingtonpost.com/sound-that-only-your-cat-can-hear/.

I: Whisker, "How Smart Are Cats?" *Litter – Robot – Blog*, posted March 11, 2019, https://www.litter-robot.com/blog/how-smart-are-cats/.

J: "Cats' Jaws," DK findout!, https://www.dkfindout.com/us/animals-and-nature/cats/cats-jaws/.

K: "Cat Reproduction: Heat Cycles, Pregnancies, and More," *BondVet*, August 12, 2020. https://bondvet.com/b/cat-reproduction

L: Kruzer, Adrienne. "Litter Box Basics Every Cat Owner Should Know," *The Spruce Pets*, updated March 17, 2021, https://www.thesprucepets.com/litter-box-basics-every-cat-owner-should-know-4688914.

M: Kjørstad, Elise, journalist. Nuse, Ingrid P., English version. "Your Cat Meows Mostly for You," sciencenorway.no, October 17, 2019, https://sciencenorway.no/animal-kingdom-communication/your-cat-meows-mostly-for-you/1578244.

N: Young, Sarah. "Cats Are Just As Loyal To Their Owners As Dogs, Study Finds," *Independent*, September 24, 2019, https://www.independent.co.uk/life-style/cats-loyal-owners-dogs-behaviour-myth-a9118496.html.

O: "The Importance of a Clean Litter Box," *Pet and Dog Care*, Richell, December 30, 2020, https://www.richellusa.com/the-importance-of-a-clean-litter-box/.

P: Fields, Lisa. "Why Do Cats Purr?," *Fetch by WebMD*, Reviewed by Amy Flowers, DVM on May 08, 2021, https://pets.webmd.com/cats/why-do-cats-purr.

Q: "How Fast Can a Cat Run, How High Can a Cat Jump & More!," *Cats, Cat Behavior And Training*, petfinder, Purina. https://www.petfinder.com/cats/cat-behavior-and-training/how-fast-cats-run-how-high-cats-jump/.

R: "Why Are Cats' Tongues Rough?," *Wonderopolis*, https://www.wonderopolis.org/wonder/why-are-cats-tongues-rough.

S: "Sphynx/Hairless Cat," *Cat Breeds*, petfinder, Nutrina, https://www.petfinder.com/cat-breeds/sphynx/.

T: "How Many Toes Do Cats Have?," *Catological*, https://www.catological.com/cat-toes/.

U: "Ask the Vet: Why Does My Cat Roll Over When He Sees Me?," *Ask the Vet*, Sunset Veterinary Clinic, https://www.sunsetvetclinic.com/ask-the-vet-why-does-my-cat-roll-over-when-he-sees-me/.

V: Gannt, Emily. "Can Cats Live Without Vaccines?," *Dog Wellness, Wag!*, edited November 17, 2021, https://wagwalking.com/wellness/can-cats-live-without-vaccines.

W: Buzhardt, Lynn DVM. "Why Do Cats Have Whiskers?," *Know Your Pet*, VCA Animal Hospitals, https://vcahospitals.com/know-your-pet/why-do-cats-have-whiskers.

X: "Grand Titled Cats in the UK," Roll of Honour, Norwegian Forest Cat Club, https://www.nfcc.co.uk/grand-titled-cats-in-the-uk.

Y: "The Maine Coon Cat," *Breeds*, The Cat Fanciers' Association, https://cfa.org/maine-coon-cat/.

Z: "Zibeline Cat," *Cat Chit Chat*, Blogger, posted June 5, 2021, https://cat-chitchat.pictures-of-cats.org/2021/06/zibeline-cat.html.